N(

WORLD HERITAGE

Protecting Earth's History

Brendan and Debbie Gallagher

This edition first published in 2011 in the United States of America by Smart Apple Media. All rights reserved. No part of this book may be reproduced in any form or by any means without written permission from the publisher.

Smart Apple Media
P.O. Box 3263
Mankato, MN, 56002

First published in 2010 by
MACMILLAN EDUCATION AUSTRALIA PTY LTD
15–19 Claremont St, South Yarra, Australia 3141

Visit our web site at www.macmillan.com.au or go directly to www.macmillanlibrary.com.au

Associated companies and representatives throughout the world.

Copyright © Brendan and Debbie Gallagher 2010

Library of Congress Cataloging-in-Publication Data

Gallagher, Brendan.
    Protecting earth's history : Brendan and Debbie Gallagher.
       p. cm. — (World heritage)
    Includes index.
    ISBN 978-1-59920-578-6 (library bound)
    1. National parks and reserves—Juvenile literature. 2. Environmental protection—Juvenile literature. I. Gallagher, Debbie, 1969– II. Title.
    SB481.3.G35 2011
    333.78'3—dc22
                                            2009053008

Publisher: Carmel Heron
Managing Editor: Vanessa Lanaway
Editor: Kirstie Innes-Will
Proofreader: Paige Amor
Designer: Kerri Wilson
Page layout: Kerri Wilson
Photo researcher: Legend Images
Illustrator: Guy Holt
Production Controller: Vanessa Johnson

Manufactured in China by Macmillan Production (Asia) Ltd.
Kwun Tong, Kowloon, Hong Kong
Supplier Code: CP December 2009

Acknowledgments
The author and the publisher are grateful to the following for permission to reproduce copyright material:

Cover photograph of Toroweap Point, Grand Canyon © Anton Foltin/iStockphoto

Photographs courtesy of:
© Liu Liqun/Corbis, 25; © Roger Ressmeyer/Corbis, 14; © George Steinmetz/Corbis, 16; © Gerald Cubitt, 17; © Michael Fischer/Dreamstime.com, 26; © Goncaloferreira/Dreamstime.com, 7; Greg Vaughn/Getty Images, 15; © Anton Foltin/iStockphoto, 1; © Paul Morton/iStockphoto, 23; © Jan Rihak/iStockphoto, 11; © 2008 Jupiterimages Corporation, 9; Etienne Laliberté, 20; Image Science and Analysis Laboratory, NASA-Johnson Space Center, «The Gateway to Astronaut Photography of Earth», 28; © Pete Oxford/naturepl.com, 24; Miguasha Prince: Parc national de Miguasha - Oeil pour Oeil – Sépaq, 21; Photolibrary/Peter Harrison, 10; © Albo/Shutterstock, 13; © blueee/Shutterstock, 27; © Sebastien Burel/Shutterstock, 18; © John Carnemolla/Shutterstock, 22; © graham s. klotz/Shutterstock, 19; © Mary Lane/Shutterstock, 8; © Xavier Marchant/Shutterstock, 12; © Vladimir Melnik/Shutterstock, 6; Gregory S. Springer, 29; leaf/stockxpert, 31; Wikimedia Commons photo by Michael David Hill, 30.

While every care has been taken to trace and acknowledge copyright, the publisher tenders their apologies for any accidental infringement where copyright has proved untraceable. Where the attempt has been unsuccessful, the publisher welcomes information that would redress the situation.

Please note
At the time of printing, the Internet addresses appearing in this book were correct. Owing to the dynamic nature of the Internet, however, we cannot guarantee that all these addresses will remain correct.

Contents

When a word in the text is printed in **bold,** look for its meaning in the glossary boxes.

World Heritage

There are places around the world that are important to all peoples. We call these places the world's heritage. Some of these places are human creations, such as the pyramids of Egypt. Some are natural creations, such as the Great Barrier Reef of Australia.

The World Heritage List

The World Heritage List is a list of **sites** that must be protected because they have some kind of outstanding importance for the world. This list was created in 1972, and new places are added every year. Each site on the World Heritage List belongs to one of the following categories:

 NATURAL – for example, waterfalls, forests or deserts

 CULTURAL – for example, a building or a site where an event occurred

 MIXED – if it has both natural and cultural features

UNESCO

UNESCO, the United Nations Educational, Scientific, and Cultural Organization, is the organization that maintains the World Heritage List. Find out more at www.unesco.org.

World Heritage Criteria

A place can be **inscribed** on the World Heritage List if it meets at least one of these ten **criteria** and is an outstanding example of it. The criteria are:

 i a masterpiece of human creative genius

 ii a site representing the sharing of human ideas

 iii a site representing a special culture or civilization

 iv a historical building or landscape from a period of history

 v a site representing or important to a traditional culture

 vi a site representing an important event, idea, living tradition, or belief

 vii a very beautiful or unique natural site

 viii a site showing evidence of Earth's history

 ix an important ecosystem

 x an important natural habitat for species protection

KEY TERMS

sites	places
inscribed	added to
criteria	rules or requirements

4

Protecting Earth's History

Protecting Earth's History is about protecting places that show how Earth has changed over thousands and millions of years. The continents of Earth were once all connected to each other, but Earth never stays the same – it is always changing. It changes very, very slowly, but, over millions of years, these changes make huge differences. Now there are several continents instead of just one. Protecting Earth's history means protecting the places that best show how the physical features of Earth and the **species** that live on it have changed over millions of years.

Criteria for Protecting Earth's History

Many of the places in this book are important for many reasons. This book focuses on just one reason: how a place shows an important stage in Earth's history. This is reason viii on the list of reasons for being on the World Heritage List.

Protecting World Heritage

Governments around the world have all agreed to protect the sites on the World Heritage List. A site that is not being properly looked after may be put on the List of World Heritage in Danger. See http://whc.unesco.org/en/158/

This map shows the location of the World Heritage sites covered in this book.

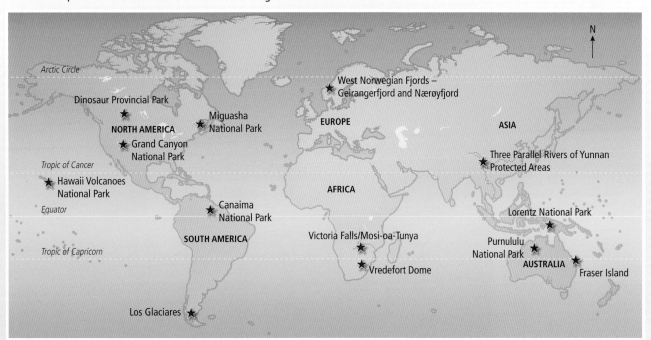

species   groups of plants or animals that have something in common

Canaima National Park

Canaima National Park in Venezuela is a series of table-topped mountains, called tepuis, surrounded by valleys of **savanna** and forests. The tepuis are made of sandstone and they run across the landscape like a string of islands in the ocean.

FACT FILE

VENEZUELA

Canaima National Park protects evidence – in the tepuis – of the landmass known as **Gondwana**.

Category:

Criteria:

tepui

flat tops

waterfall

cliff face

savanna

Angel Falls, the highest waterfall in the world, falls from the tepui called Auyuntepui.

TIMELINE

1,700 million years ago
Some rock forms in the park are already formed.

1962
Canaima is made a national park.

1994
The site is inscribed on the World Heritage List.

Important Features

The tepuis were once part of a flat landscape. However, over millions of years water and wind **eroded** the landscape, leaving behind only the harder parts, which are the tepuis. Rainfall continues to erode the tepuis as it drains off the tops, creating hundreds of waterfalls. Tepuis only exist in this region of the world, but they show similarities to rock formations in the west of Africa. They are evidence of the time in Earth's history when Africa and South America belonged to Gondwana.

Issues

The highest of the tepuis is Roraima. Most of Roraima is within the territory of Venezuela. However, Brazil owns part of it, and goldmining there has destroyed much of the rock. There is pressure to allow mining in Canaima National Park as it too contains important minerals.

Did You Know?
Angel Falls is 3,212 feet (979 meters) high, making it just over three times the height of the Eiffel Tower.

The tepuis are between 3,280 and 6,560 feet (1,000 and 2,000 m) high.

GLOSSARY

savanna	flat, grassy plains with few trees
Gondwana	large, ancient continent which was made up of what are now Africa, South America, Antarctica, and Australia
eroded	wore away

Dinosaur Provincial Park

Dinosaur Provincial Park is an area of deeply **eroded**, bare land in central Canada. The **fossils** of at least 37 different dinosaur species have been discovered there. The fossils date from a time known as the Age of Reptiles. No other place in the world has the same quality or variety of dinosaur fossils.

FACT FILE

CANADA

The Dinosaur Provincial Park protects evidence of the Age of Reptiles.

Category:

Criteria:

The dinosaur fossils come from a 17-mile (27-kilometer) stretch along the Red Deer River.

fossil sites

eroded, bare land

TIMELINE

75 million years ago
The area is a forest, and the fossils are formed.

1882
John Ware discovers fossils in the area.

1955
The site is inscribed on the World Heritage List.

1979
Dinosaur Provincial Park is established.

These dinosaur bones were found in a piece of rock from Dinosaur Provincial Park.

Important Features

The Dinosaur Provincial Park was once a forest, with great rivers flowing through it. Dinosaurs like the Daspletosaurus lived there. Its name means "frightful lizard" and it was a fierce dinosaur that probably attacked and ate other dinosaurs. Fossils of the Daspletosaurus have only been discovered at the Dinosaur Provincial Park.

Issues

The most serious problem facing Dinosaur Provincial Park is visitors removing fossils from the area. Some fossils are loose and can be easily removed, while others have been dug out of the rocks. Park officers are trying to educate visitors not to take these precious rocks.

Did You Know?
The fossils at Dinosaur Provincial Park were discovered by a former slave from the southern United States.

GLOSSARY

eroded	worn away
fossils	hardened remains of an animal or plant found in rock

Fraser Island

Fraser Island, off the east coast of Australia, is the largest sand island in the world. Some of the sand dunes on the island are more than 700,000 years old. The island is an outstanding place to learn about sand dunes.

FACT FILE

AUSTRALIA

Fraser Island protects evidence of how dunes are formed.

Category:

Criteria:

More than 100 lakes are found among the unique sand dunes of Fraser Island.

sand dunes

lake

rain forest

TIMELINE

2 million years ago	700,000 years ago	1908	1971	1992
Ocean currents begin depositing sand in the area.	Huge sand dunes start to form.	Part of Fraser Island is made a forestry reserve.	The Great Sandy National Park, including Fraser Island, is established.	Fraser Island is inscribed on the World Heritage List.

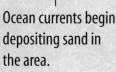

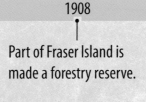

Important Features

Fraser Island was formed on a low-lying land area created by volcanic activity. Ocean currents deposited sand in the area from the Australian continent and from the **erosion** of massive mountains on Antarctica. This happened when Australia and Antarctica were part of the same landmass, known as **Gondwana**. The process continued over thousands of years creating mounds of sand up to 747 feet (240 meters) high. **Rain forests** now cover much of Fraser Island.

> ### Did You Know?
> Fraser Island is the only place in the world where rain forests grow on sand dunes.

Issues

Environmental groups are calling for Fraser Island to be placed on the List of World Heritage in Danger. They are concerned that tourist vehicles in the park are polluting the lakes. They believe that sandy tracks near the lakes need to be closed in order to protect the environment.

Four-wheel driving on Fraser Island is very popular, but the island's ecosystem must also be protected.

GLOSSARY

erosion	the process of being worn away
Gondwana	the large, ancient continent which was made up of what are now Africa, South America, Antarctica, and Australia
rain forests	forests that receive a lot of rainfall

Grand Canyon National Park

Grand Canyon National Park is a dry landscape with a huge **canyon** nearly 4,920 feet (1,500 meters) deep. The canyon was carved from the surrounding landscape by the **eroding** power of the Colorado River.

FACT FILE

UNITED STATES

The Grand Canyon National Park protects evidence of nearly 2,000 million years of Earth's history.

Category:

Criteria:

The Colorado River continues to deepen the Grand Canyon, revealing older rock forms below the surface.

Colorado River

dry landscape

layers of rock

TIMELINE

1,840 million years ago	1919	1963	1979	2008

The oldest rocks at the Grand Canyon form.

The Grand Canyon becomes a national park.

Glen Canyon Dam is built.

The site is inscribed on the World Heritage List.

Large volumes of water are released from Glen Canyon Dam.

Important Features

By cutting through the landscape, the Colorado River has exposed the rock walls of the Grand Canyon. The walls show different layers of rock. Each layer took millions of years to form.

Issues

Since Glen Canyon Dam was built, the summer flow of the Colorado River has been 10 percent of its previous volume. This has badly affected plants and animals, as well as the landscape. In 2008, water was released from the dam into the river, in a test, to try and restore the natural **ecosystem**. More tests will be carried out in the future.

Did You Know?
The Grand Canyon is about 277 miles (446 kilometers) long and between 656 feet (200 m) and 19 miles (30 km) wide.

Layers in the rock show a timeline of changes on Earth. This is a unique example of the way landscapes form over millions of years.

GLOSSARY

canyon	a deep valley with steep sides
eroding	wearing away
ecosystem	a community of plants and animals

Hawaii Volcanoes National Park

Hawaii Volcanoes National Park is a volcanic landscape on Hawai'i, the more southerly of the islands of Hawaii. The park contains two of the most active volcanoes in the world, Kilauea and Mauna Loa.

FACT FILE

HAWAII (UNITED STATES)

Hawai'i

Hawaii Volcanoes National Park protects evidence of how volcanoes form islands.

Category:

Criteria:

Kilauea is the most active volcano in the world and it continues to help form Hawai'i.

Pacific Ocean

lava

lower part of Mount Kilauea

TIMELINE

460,000 years ago
Volcanic activity begins to create the island of Hawai'i.

1916
The area is made a national park.

1987
The site is inscribed on the World Heritage List.

Important Features

The flowing of **lava** from the volcanoes is constantly changing the landscape and enlarging the island. Kilauea is the newest volcano in the park. In 2008, there was a small eruption at the peak, but most of the volcanic activity occurs at an opening on the side. Mauna Loa is much bigger than Kilauea and it is one of the best examples of a shield volcano in the world. Shield volcanoes are flat rather than cone shaped. Mauna Loa rises 13,680 feet (4,170 meters) above sea level and reaches to the ocean floor 16,400 feet (5,000 m) below.

Issues

Grasses from Africa and South America were introduced to Hawai'i to feed cattle and sheep. However, these grasses have also found their way into the national park, where they are replacing native species. Park managers are trying to remove the grasses while protecting unspoiled areas.

Did You Know?

Mauna Loa is the largest volcano on Earth, covering just over half the island of Hawai'i.

Mauna Loa is a shield volcano. It is built upon layer after layer of hardened lava.

GLOSSARY

lava   hot, melted rock

Lorentz National Park

Lorentz National Park in Indonesia is a **tropical** area. It runs 93 miles (150 kilometers) from the Arafura Sea, through swampy **lowlands** to the high mountains of New Guinea. Below this area two **tectonic plates** are colliding, an important process in Earth's history.

FACT FILE

INDONESIA

Lorentz National Park protects evidence of how tectonic plates form mountains.

Category:

Criteria:

The mountain range in Lorentz includes the highest peak in Southeast Asia, Puncak Jaya, at 16,024 feet (4,884 meters).

Puncak Jaya

mountains pushed up by tectonic activity

snow

TIMELINE

25 million years ago
The tectonic plates under Australia and the Pacific collide and mountains begin to form.

1978
Lorentz is made a nature reserve.

1997
Lorentz is declared a national park.

1999
The site is inscribed on the World Heritage List.

Important Features

The collision of the tectonic plates raised the island of New Guinea from under the sea. The Pacific plate is sliding under the Australian plate and this action pushed up a mountain range, which is still forming. **Glaciers** formed on the mountains, shaping them. Lorentz is the only World Heritage site to contain both **marine** areas and glaciers.

Issues

In 2008, a UNESCO mission discovered that a road was being built through the park, damaging the landscape. The park authorities have been asked to stop the road being built. If a road is to be built in a World Heritage area, it is important to study the impact on the environment and landscape first.

Puncak Jaya is one of the few tropical places where glaciers are found.

Did You Know?
Lorentz is one of only three tropical places on Earth to have glaciers.

GLOSSARY

tropical	from the hot and humid area between the Tropic of Cancer and the Tropic of Capricorn
lowlands	areas that are not high above sea level
tectonic plates	huge sections of the Earth's crust
glaciers	rivers of packed ice that move very slowly
marine	of the ocean

Los Glaciares

Los Glaciares is an **alpine** landscape on the eastern edge of the large ice field in Patagonia, a region of southern Argentina and Chile. About half of Los Glaciares is covered by the ice field, and it includes many **glaciers**, which begin at an **altitude** of 4,920 feet (1,500 meters).

FACT FILE

CHILE ARGENTINA

Los Glaciares protects evidence of the way glaciers form landscapes.

Category:

Criteria:

The glaciers of Los Glaciares form above a landscape of lakes, forests, and grassy plains.

ice cap

glacier

forest

grassy plains

TIMELINE

100,000 years ago	1937	1945	1981
Glaciers begin forming in the Los Glaciares area.	Los Glaciares is made a protected area.	Los Glaciares is made a national park.	Los Glaciares is inscribed on the World Heritage List.

The famous Perito Moreno glacier is 3 miles (5 kilometers) wide and rises 197 feet (60 m) above Lake Argentino.

Important Features

From the ice cap in the mountains above them, 13 large glaciers run through the park, shaping the valley. Perhaps the most well-known glacier of Los Glaciares is Perito Moreno. Every few years, large chunks of ice break off the tip of this glacier and fall into Lake Argentino as icebergs.

Did You Know?

As well as the 13 large glaciers, there are more than 200 smaller glaciers in Los Glaciares.

Issues

The Upsala glacier at Los Glaciares is 37 miles (60 km) in length and it is the longest in South America. However, it is losing about 46 feet (14 m) a year because of **global warming**. Between 1975 and 2000, melting waters from Los Glaciares made up about 10 percent of the world's total melting waters from glaciers. This melting water is raising sea levels.

GLOSSARY

alpine	high, mountainous
glaciers	rivers of packed ice that move very slowly
altitude	height above sea level
global warming	increases in temperatures on Earth

Miguasha National Park

Miguasha National Park is a coastal area at the mouth of the Ristigouche River in Canada. The park contains numerous fish **fossils** from a period of history known as the Devonian Period, or the Age of Fishes. The Devonian Period was a time when no large animals lived on land.

Miguasha's fish fossils, evidence of the Devonian Period, are found in this cliff on the Ristigouche River.

cliff

Ristigouche River

beach

TIMELINE

415 to 350 million years ago	1880	1985	1999
In the Devonian Period, the fish fossils form.	The fossils at Miguasha are discovered.	Miguasha is made a national park.	The site is inscribed on the World Heritage List.

Important Features

Miguasha National Park protects a land formation that is rich in fossils. It runs 5 miles (8 kilometers) along the north bank of the Ristigouche River. During the Devonian Period, Miguasha was located near the equator. It was part of an area where a wide river met the sea, and it was filled with a huge variety of fish. Some of the fish had bones and muscles in their fins. These fish were able to use their fins to crawl along.

This fossil is called the Prince of Miguasha.

Issues

There are many visitors to Miguasha National Park, but it is well protected. Visitors to the park are asked not to take rocks from the cliff or from the beach. They are also asked to return any fossils they might find. No mining is allowed in and around the park area.

GLOSSARY

fossils	hardened remains of an animal or plant found in rock

Purnululu National Park

Purnululu National Park is a **plateau** that rises more than 656 feet (200 meters) above a dry **savanna** landscape in the northwest of Australia. For 20 million years, air and water have been slowly **eroding** the plateau, creating **gorges** and huge domed rocks.

FACT FILE

AUSTRALIA

Purnululu National Park protects an excellent example of the power of **erosion**.

Category:

Criteria:

The plateau of Purnululu is about 22 miles (35 kilometers) by 15 miles (24 km) in area. It took millions of years to form.

savanna

plateau

domed rocks

TIMELINE

20 million years ago
The erosion of the mountain range begins.

1997
Purnululu is made a national park.

2003
Purnululu National Park is inscribed on the World Heritage List.

Important Features

Purnululu is warm and dry from April to October, and very hot and wet from November to March. Heavy rainfall creates fast-moving rivers, pools of water, and waterfalls. The water flow is slowly but constantly changing the landscape. Dark gray bands form around the domes. These are actually tiny plants, called algae, which live on the surface of the rocks.

Issues

The biggest problem facing Purnululu National Park is **introduced species**. Large numbers of cattle and donkeys have damaged vegetation in the park. The park managers are working to keep cattle and other animals, such as cats, out of the park.

The orange bands in the rocks get their color from iron and manganese (a metallic element).

> **Did You Know?**
> Between 1975 and 2000, park authorities removed 25,000 cattle and 4,000 donkeys from the area.

GLOSSARY

plateau	a wide, flat area in a high place
savanna	a flat, grassy plain with few trees
eroding	wearing away
gorges	canyons
erosion	the process of being worn away
introduced species	plants or animals that are not native to the area

Three Parallel Rivers of Yunnan Protected Areas

Three Parallel Rivers of Yunnan Protected Areas is a mountainous area in China. Here three great rivers – the Yangtze, the Mekong, and the Salween – flow north to south over 186 miles (300 kilometers), forming deep **gorges**. The rock formations of the area show 50 million years of Earth's history.

FACT FILE

CHINA

The Three Parallel Rivers of Yunnan site protects evidence of how mountains form.

Category:

Criteria:

mountains

gorge

Salween River

The extremely deep gorges of the Three Parallel Rivers of Yunnan are incredible landforms.

TIMELINE

50 million years ago	1988	2003
The gorges of the Three Parallel Rivers begin to form.	The area is named a scenic attraction by the Chinese government.	Three Parallel Rivers of Yunnan Protected Areas is inscribed on the World Heritage List.

Tiger Leaping Gorge in Yunnan is one of the longest, deepest, and narrowest gorges in the world.

Important Features

Two **tectonic plates**, the Eurasian plate and the Indian plate, collide in this area. The collision pushed up the Himalayas, as well as the area of the Three Parallel Rivers. This caused the rivers to flow more powerfully, **eroding** the landscape and creating the gorges, which are 2 miles (3 km) deep in places. Mountain peaks around the gorges are up to 4 miles (6 km) high.

Issues

One threat to the site is the planned building of **hydro-electric** power stations on the rivers. Hydro-electric power stations change the flow of water in a river. This affects the natural eroding processes of the rivers.

GLOSSARY

gorges	canyons
tectonic plates	huge sections of the Earth's crust
eroding	wearing away
hydro-electric	using water to produce electricity

Victoria Falls/ Mosi-oa-Tunya

Victoria Falls/Mosi-oa-Tunya, on the border of Zambia and Zimbabwe, is one of the largest waterfalls on Earth. The local people, the Kololo, call the falls *Mosi-oa-Tunya*, meaning "the smoke that thunders." This is because of the enormous mist that comes off the waterfall and forms **rain forest** around it.

FACT FILE

ZAMBIA
ZIMBABWE
AFRICA

Victoria Falls/Mosi-oa-Tunya protects an outstanding example of the power of water.

Category: 🌳

Criteria: ⛰️ 🌐

Mosi-oa-Tunya, one of the largest waterfalls in the world, is 5,600 feet (1,700 meters) wide and more than 360 feet (108 m) high.

gorges

Mosi-oa-Tunya

rain forest mist

Zambezi River

TIMELINE

2 million years ago	1855	1952	1989	2001	2007
The Zambezi River starts creating gorges.	Scottish explorer Dr David Livingstone calls Mosi-oa-Tunya Victoria Falls after Queen Victoria.	Victoria Falls National Park is established.	The site is inscribed on the World Heritage List.	Hotels are built at Mosi-oa-Tunya.	The Zambian government decides not to allow a new hotel at Mosi-oa-Tunya.

Up to 132 million gallons (500 million liters) of water per second flow over the waterfall.

Important Features

The Zambezi River has carved its way through the landscape for 2 million years, creating a series of gorges. Each gorge that is downstream from the waterfalls was once a location of the waterfall. However, as the river **eroded** the landscape, the location of Mosi-oa-Tunya moved upstream.

Issues

The most serious issue facing Mosi-oa-Tunya is tourism. Hotels built near the waterfall have a negative impact on the natural environment. Elephants that cross the river can be blocked by these buildings and by electric fences. Three elephants were swept over the falls in 2007. There are plans for more hotels in the area.

Did You Know?
Mosi-oa-Tunya is Zambia's only World Heritage site.

GLOSSARY

rain forest	a forest that receives a lot of rainfall
eroded	wore away

Vredefort Dome

Vredefort Dome is a crater that is 263 miles (380 kilometers) wide in the east of South Africa. The crater was created 2,000 million years ago when a 6-mile (10-km) wide **meteorite** crashed into Earth's surface.

FACT FILE

SOUTH AFRICA

Vredefort Dome protects the clearest example of the **impact** of a meteorite on Earth.

Category:

Criteria:

As this satellite image shows, Vredefort Dome is so large it can be seen from space.

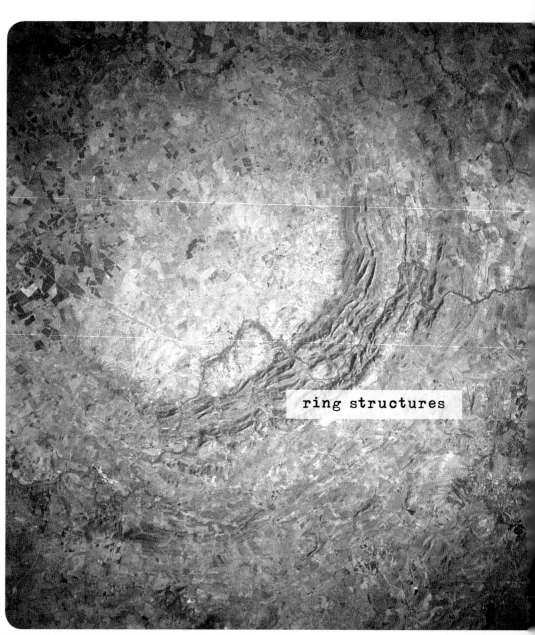

ring structures

TIMELINE

2,023 million years ago
A meteorite crashes into Earth in South Africa, creating a dent in Earth.

2002
The dome is declared a national heritage site.

2005
Vredefort Dome is inscribed on the World Heritage List.

Important Features

Vredefort Dome is the oldest and largest meteorite impact crater on Earth. The meteorite set off the greatest explosion ever witnessed on Earth. Rocks on the surface melted in the heat. Rocks further away cracked and split. Over time, Vredefort Dome has **eroded**, allowing scientists to see more of the unusual rock formations.

Issues

Visitors to the dome have damaged some of the area's unusual rock forms. Other visitors have taken loose rocks as souvenirs. Some of the rock formations may need to be placed under permanent protection to prevent further damage and theft.

Did You Know?

The force of the meteorite at Vredefort was 5,000 million times more powerful than the bomb dropped on the city of Hiroshima, Japan in 1945.

The impact of the meteorite at Vredefort created a dent in Earth, pushing up the surrounding area.

GLOSSARY

meteorite	a mass of stone or metal that has reached Earth from outer space
impact	the force of one object hitting another
eroded	worn away

West Norwegian Fjords — Geirangerfjord and Nærøyfjord

West Norwegian Fjords – Geirangerfjord and Nærøyfjord in Norway are two of the world's longest and deepest **fjords**. During **ice ages,** the fjords were created by **glaciers** that filled the valleys, shaping them.

The fjords were originally shaped by glaciers and now are filled with water and have waterfalls. The two most famous waterfalls on Geirangerfjord are the Seven Sisters and Wooer waterfalls.

Seven Sisters waterfalls

glacier-shaped sides

water-filled valley

TIMELINE

1 million to 10,000 years ago	1970	1984	2005
During a series of ice ages, glaciers form, creating deep, round valleys.	All important natural features are given protection in Norway.	Part of the area is made a nature reserve.	The site is inscribed on the World Heritage List.

Important Features

Over the past million years, more than forty ice ages have occurred on Earth. In Norway, glaciers formed and moved through the landscape, creating deep, round, valleys. As sea levels rose at the end of the ice ages, the water flooded the valleys, forming fjords. The two fjords are up to 1.5 miles (2.5 kilometers) wide, with the cliff sides rising up to 4,590 feet (1,400 meters) above the water.

Did You Know?

The name of Nærøyfjord comes from the name of the Norse god of the sea, Njord.

Issues

Most of the 200 fjords in Norway have been affected by human activities, such as the building of **hydro-electric** dams. These two west Norwegian fjords are protected from such human activities. Plans for a military base in the area were abandoned when the fjords became a World Heritage site.

Nærøyfjord is the narrowest fjord in the world, with one part only 820 feet (250 m) wide.

GLOSSARY

fjords	narrow, deep inlets from the sea that flow between steep mountain sides or cliffs
ice ages	times in history when Earth was covered by large ice sheets
glaciers	rivers of packed ice that move very slowly
hydro-electric	using water to produce electricity

Index